BIG QUESTIONS:

HOW DO I KNOW GOD EXISTS?

NASHVILLE, TENNESSEE

Big Questions: How Do I Know God Exists?

Printed in China
1 2 3 4 5 6 24 23 22 21
RRD

Contents

Introduction . . . 3
What Do I Do with My Doubts? . . . 5
Does the Cosmological Argument Show There Is a God? . . . 13
Does the Design Argument Show There Is a God? . . . 17
Does the Existence of the Mind Provide Evidence for God? . . . 21
Does the Moral Argument Show There Is a God? . . . 25
Can Something Be True for You and Not for Me? . . . 29
If God Made the Universe, Who Made God? . . . 34
Is the Old Testament Trustworthy? . . . 37
Is the Old Testament Ethical? . . . 45
Is the New Testament Trustworthy? . . . 51
Has Historical Criticism Proved the Bible False? . . . 57
Are Miracles Believable? . . . 63
Did Jesus Really Rise from the Dead? . . . 66
Can Naturalistic Theories Account for the Resurrection? . . 73

INTRODUCTION

One doesn't typically hear the word *apologetics* in the everyday vernacular of Christians today. The term is derived from a Greek word meaning "a defense." Thus, engaging in Christian apologetics simply means providing a Christian defense of the faith. Or, to say it another way, it involves giving an intellectual defense of *why* we believe *what* we believe.

The apostle Peter writes, "But in your hearts regard Christ the Lord as holy, ready at any time to give a defense to anyone who asks you for a reason for the hope that is in you" (1Pt 3:15). Peter, along with other writers of Scripture, knew the importance of being able to offer reasons to others regarding our belief in Christ or the Christian worldview in general. If asked why we believe any tenet of biblical doctrine, Christians ought to be able to give coherent reasons for that belief.

But not only does apologetics help us to defend our beliefs, it is also helps us to strengthen the faith we have—to bolster it, to assure us that our beliefs are in fact reasonable. This means that apologetics isn't merely a mental exercise for thinking deeply and critically about matters. Instead, it is another discipline of the Christian life that helps increase our love for and devotion to God as we seek to know him and make him better known to others.

The Big Questions series serves these two purposes for the reader. It provides reasons and evidence on select topics to both strengthen Christian faith and to help one articulate that faith to others. Curated from the *Apologetics Study Bible* and *Worldview Study Bible*, the content in this booklet will equip you in your journey toward being better grounded in your faith and better equipped at sharing it.

— *Andy McLean*

WHAT DO I DO WITH MY DOUBTS?

Andy McLean

The experience of addressing difficult questions or seeking to overcome doubts isn't uncommon—even among Christians. This shouldn't come as a surprise for the simple reason that we, unlike God, are finite creatures who don't possess infinite knowledge. Because we don't know everything, doubts can sometimes arise.

Yet despite the reality of many Christians moving through seasons of doubt in the discipleship process, it is also common for many churches to not know how to properly address the doubts and difficult questions that come their way from among their fellow Christians.

In fact, in many circles having personal doubts is often viewed as taboo, which only adds to the shame a fellow Christian feels when he or she is wrestling with them. What is needed instead is a church culture and environment that fosters an atmosphere where people can express their doubts and ask the questions that need to be addressed in order to achieve the mental peace they seek. But in order to do just that, let's explore the subject of doubts a little more in depth to better help both ourselves and others navigate this terrain when seasons of doubt arise.

How the Bible Deals with Those Who Doubt

It is important to recognize that faith and doubt are not necessarily opposites. Doubting is not unbelief, although not dealing with one's doubts may eventually lead to a place of unbelief. When a fellow Christian is wrestling with some form of doubting, it is important to help that person adequately address those doubts so that he or she can continue to grow and flourish in their Christian faith.

While there are certainly other instances of people in the Bible who experienced doubt, let's look at two familiar characters and what they teach us about how we might respond to doubts in our own lives.

In Luke 7:18–23, we come across a scene where John the Baptist, imprisoned by Herod, began to struggle with his faith in light of his circumstances. So much so that he sent some of his disciples to Jesus for confirmation that he was, in fact, who John believed him to be—the Messiah. Instead of Jesus being discouraged by this or chiding John for his lack of faith, Jesus graciously replied with reasons and evidences that, in the end, give assurance. Jesus told John the things that were taking place as a result of his ministry, such as the blind being able to see, the lame to walk, and the dead raised to life. The specific works Jesus was doing would have been reassuring to John not only because they were supernatural works of God, but also because they were fulfilling the Old Testament prophecies regarding the works of the Messiah who was to come.

Another case study, and perhaps the most well-known instance of doubt in the minds of many, is that of Thomas the disciple. In fact, it is unfortunate that Thomas is not remembered for some of the good things he said and did in the Gospels, but instead is known as the doubting disciple. After all, Thomas displayed outstanding courage and an overall willingness to be a martyr alongside of Jesus in John 11. Of course, there was nothing necessarily wrong on Thomas's part with wanting to see the evidences for Jesus's resurrection (he wasn't present when Jesus first appeared to the other disciples). We know this because, at the very least, Jesus didn't correct Thomas on this point (Jn 20:24–29). Remember, the other disciples did not believe Mary Magdalene when she told them Jesus had been resurrected until they saw him themselves. So, unlike his peers, Thomas wasn't afforded the opportunity they had to witness with his own eyes and with his own hands the bodily resurrection of Jesus.

The question here isn't so much the issue of doubting but rather: Did he really need to see in order to believe? In other words, did Thomas, much like us today, still have ample reason to believe the claims apart from witnessing the miracle of the resurrection. The answer is an emphatic yes! After all, Thomas had been with Jesus for the previous three years of his ministry and witnessed all that Jesus had done. He even heard Jesus declare that he would, eventually, be put to death and rise again.

Not only that but Thomas also knew the character of his friends who reported to him that Jesus had returned. He lived with them, served with them, shared countless meals with them, and knew the type of men they were and the character they possessed. All of these reasons, and many more, should have been sufficient for Thomas to believe that the resurrection of Jesus, as told by his friends, was true.

In the end, Jesus didn't chide Thomas or John for asking the questions or wanting to see the evidence. Instead, in both cases Jesus responded and graciously gave them the evidence they needed. While we might not be afforded the same opportunity as Thomas in seeing Jesus's bodily resurrection, Jesus still invites us, as he did with Thomas, to consider the overwhelming evidence that remains. Like Thomas, we too can look to Jesus's life and ministry for confirmation of our faith; we can also look to the faithful witness of the disciples as deserving of our trust. And when we do that, Jesus says of us, "Blessed are those who have not seen and yet believe" (Jn 20:29).

How to Deal with My Own Doubts

When it comes to addressing our own doubts and growing in our faith and commitment to Christ, it is important to realize that doubts come in a variety of forms, each deserving a unique response in the task of faith seeking understanding. The most common forms include the following:

1. ***Intellectual doubts:*** Intellectual doubts are what typically come to mind when people think of doubting. For instance, they come in the form of questions relating to alleged contradictions between Christianity and science, or perhaps questions pertaining to how Jesus can be both divine and human. Since these doubts are intellectual by nature, they require an intellectual response to help the person overcome any obstacles.

2. ***Emotional doubts:*** These types of doubts often arise in the midst of some tragedy or suffering. They may look like intellectual doubts on the surface, but a little deeper digging often reveals that the person is dealing with emotional struggles. For instance, someone who has recently experienced the loss of a loved one while going through a season of sorrow and spiritual depression may

begin to ask questions like, "Why would God allow such suffering and evil?", "Does God really exist, and if so, does he care?", "If God is all-good and all-powerful, why did he allow this to happen?" and so forth. Questions like these can come from a person with intellectual doubts, but when they come from a source of emotional turmoil, intellectual answers offer little to no help. At this point, what is needed is a pastoral response, and not necessarily an intellectual or theological one.

3. ***Volitional doubts:*** These types of doubts can be characterized as coming directly from a person's will. Like emotional doubts, they too can disguise themselves as intellectual in nature. For instance, if a person has been wronged by others, perhaps even by professing Christians, and finds the idea of forgiving them inconceivable, then that person may find it convenient to begin doubting Jesus's teaching on the subject. If that is the case, then neither an intellectual response nor a pastoral response is likely to help. Here the person will need to be confronted with their heart issues of pride, authority, and their personal need of repentance, realizing that the same forgiveness that has been extended to us

should be extended to those who have wronged us in some way.

It is important to think through the source of people's doubts as we engage with them. Knowing this will not only help us to address their concerns apologetically, but it will also allow us to know them better, to assess their relationship with God, and to understand how to talk with them and pray for them. After all, the Bible clearly tells us to have mercy on those who doubt (Jude 22).

The remaining chapters in this booklet will be of particular help and comfort for those wrestling with intellectual doubts—those doubts that seek to gain mental peace and reconciliation between an aspect of our faith and something that on the surface seems to be inconsistent with what we believe. Of course, even in the absence of explicit doubts, these chapters will be immensely useful for those wanting to better understand not only *what* they believe but *why* they believe it. In both cases, the topics addressed and the answers provided will help Christians grow in their faith and commitment to Jesus as they are better equipped to know and articulate what they believe to others.

DOES THE COSMOLOGICAL ARGUMENT SHOW THERE IS A GOD?*

J. P. Moreland

The cosmological argument starts with the existence of the universe and reasons to the existence of God as the best explanation of the universe. There are different forms of the argument. Two important versions are the Leibnizian and Thomist arguments, which are named, respectively, after Gottfried W. Leibniz (AD 1646–1716) and Thomas Aquinas (AD 1225–1274). In recent years a third version has become prominent, and it may be the

* Originally published in the *CSB Apologetics Study Bible* under the same title.

most effective of all: the *kalam cosmological argument*, which can be diagrammed as a series of alternatives:

Universe

Beginning	No Beginning
Caused	Uncaused
Personal	Impersonal

The defender of the argument tries to establish one horn of each dilemma and thus to argue for these three premises:

1. The universe had a beginning.
2. The beginning of the universe was caused.
3. The cause of the beginning of the universe was personal.

One philosophical argument for premise 1 involves the impossibility of creating an actual infinite number of events. For example, if you start counting 1, 2, 3, . . . , then you could count forever and never reach a time when an actual infinite amount of numbers had been counted. Your counting could continue forever but would always be finite; that is, it would have some point of ending.

If the universe had no beginning, then the number of events crossed to reach the present moment would be actually infinite because the universe would be infinite. It would be like counting to zero from negative infinity. Since one cannot have an actual infinite, then the present moment could never have arrived if the universe had no beginning. Since the present is real, it had to have been preceded by a finite past; therefore, there was a beginning or first event!

One scientific argument for premise 1 derives from the second law of thermodynamics, which in one form states that the amount of useful energy in the universe is being used up. If the universe were infinitely old, it would already have used up all its useful energy and have arrived at a temperature of absolute zero. Since there are many pockets of useful energy (for example, the sun), the universe must be finite in duration. Therefore, there was a beginning when the universe's useful energy was put into it "from the outside."

Premise 2 is confirmed by universal experience with no clear counterexamples. Alleged cases where something comes from nothing actually involve one thing coming into existence from something else (for example, lead from uranium).

Evidence for premise 3 derives from the fact that since time, space, and matter did not exist earlier than the beginning of the universe, the universe's cause had to be timeless, spaceless, and immaterial. This cause cannot be physical or subject to scientific law since all such causes presuppose time, space, and matter to exist. The universe's immaterial cause was timeless, spaceless, and had the power to spontaneously bring the world into existence without changing first to do so. (If it had to change before bringing the world into existence, then that change, not the act of bringing the world into existence, would be the first event.) Such a cause must have free will, and since only persons have free will, it is a personal Creator.

DOES THE DESIGN ARGUMENT SHOW THERE IS A GOD?*

William A. Dembski

Suppose you take a tour of the Louvre, that great museum in Paris housing one of the finest art collections in the world. As you walk through the museum, you come across a painting by someone named Leonardo da Vinci—the *Mona Lisa*. Suppose this is your first exposure to da Vinci; you hadn't heard of him or seen the *Mona Lisa* before. What could you conclude? Certainly you could conclude that da Vinci was a consummate painter. Nevertheless, just from the

* Originally published in the *CSB Apologetics Study Bible* under the same title.

Mona Lisa you couldn't conclude that da Vinci was also a consummate engineer, musician, scientist, and inventor, whose ideas were centuries ahead of their time.

The design argument is like this. It looks at certain features of the natural world and concludes that they exhibit evidence of a designing intelligence. But just as the *Mona Lisa* can tell us only so much about its creator (da Vinci), so the natural world can tell us only so much about its Creator (God). The design argument allows us reliably to conclude that a designing intelligence is behind the order and complexity of the natural world. But it cannot speak to the underlying nature of this designing intelligence (for instance, whether this intelligence is the transcendent, interpersonal, triune God of Christianity). Nor can it speak to the actions of that designing intelligence in human history. In particular, the design argument is silent about the revelation of Christ in Scripture. It follows that the design argument cannot "prove the gospel" or "compel someone into the kingdom."

Christian theologians have long recognized that the design argument is a modest argument. Even so, it is a powerful argument. Perhaps the best-known design argument is William Paley's. According to Paley, if we find a watch in a field (and thus lack all knowledge of how it arose), the adaptation of the watch's parts to telling time ensures that it is the product of an intelligence. So too, according to Paley, the marvelous adaptations of means to ends in organisms (such as the human eye with its ability to confer sight) ensure that organisms are the product of an intelligence. The theory of intelligent design—or ID as it is commonly abbreviated—updates Paley's argument in light of contemporary information theory and molecular biology, bringing the design argument squarely within science.

The implications of ID for the Christian faith are profound and revolutionary. The rise of modern science led to a vigorous attack on orthodox Christian theology. The high point of this attack came with Darwin's theory of evolution. Orthodox Christian theology has always been committed to the proposition that God by wisdom created the world. A clear implication of this proposition is that the design of the world is real. The central claim of Darwin's theory is that an unguided material process (random variation and natural selection) could account for the emergence of all biological complexity and order. In other words, Darwin appeared to show that the design of the world was unreal—that science had dispensed with any need for design. By showing that design is indispensable to our scientific understanding of the natural world, ID is breathing new life into the design argument and at the same time overturning the widespread misconception that science has disproved the Christian faith.

DOES THE EXISTENCE OF THE MIND PROVIDE EVIDENCE FOR GOD?*

J. P. Moreland

Many believe that finite (limited) minds provide evidence of a divine mind as their Creator. If we limit our options to theism and naturalism, it is hard to see how finite consciousness could result from the rearrangement of brute matter; it is easier to see how a conscious being could produce finite consciousness.

This argument assumes a commonsense understanding of conscious states such as sensations, thoughts, beliefs,

* Originally published in the *CSB Apologetics Study Bible* under the same title.

desires, and volitions. So understood, mental states are in no sense physical since they possess four features not owned by physical states:

1. There is a raw qualitative feel, or a "what it is like," to have a mental state such as a pain.
2. Many mental states have intentionality—being or aboutness—directed toward an object (for example, a thought about the moon).
3. Mental states are inner, private, and immediate to the subject having them.
4. Mental states fail to have crucial features (for instance, spatial extension and location) that characterize physical states and, in general, cannot be described using physical language.

Given that conscious states are immaterial and not physical, at least two reasons have been offered for why there can be no natural scientific explanation for the existence of conscious states:

Something from nothing. Before consciousness appeared, the universe contained nothing but aggregates of particles/waves standing in fields of forces. The naturalistic story of the cosmos's evolution involves the rearrangement of atomic parts into increasingly more complex structures according to natural law. Matter is brute, mechanical, physical stuff. The emergence of consciousness seems to be a case of getting something from nothing. In general, physicochemical reactions do not generate consciousness. Some say they do in the brain, yet brains seem similar to other parts of organisms' bodies (e.g., both are collections of cells totally describable in physical terms). How can like causes produce radically different effects? The appearance of the mind is utterly unpredictable and inexplicable. This radical discontinuity seems like a rupture in the natural world.

The inadequacy of evolutionary explanations. Naturalists claim that evolutionary explanations can be provided for the appearance of all organisms and their parts. In principle, an evolutionary account could be given for increasingly complex physical structures that constitute different organisms. It is clear that as long as an organism, when receiving certain inputs, generates the correct behavioral outputs under the demands of reproductive advantage, the organism will survive. What goes on inside the organism is irrelevant and becomes significant for the processes of evolution only when an output is produced. Strictly speaking, it is the output, not what caused it, that impacts the struggle for reproductive advantage. Moreover, the functions organisms carry out consciously could just as well have been done unconsciously. Thus both the sheer existence of conscious states and the precise mental content that constitutes them is outside the pale of evolutionary explanation.

It will not do to claim that consciousness simply emerged from matter when it reached a certain level of complexity, because "emergence" is merely a label for, and not an explanation of, the phenomena to be explained.

DOES THE MORAL ARGUMENT SHOW THERE IS A GOD?*

Paul Copan

Here's a good rule of thumb about morality: *Never believe those who say murder or rape may not really be wrong.* Such people haven't looked deeply enough into the basis for moral belief—and just aren't functioning properly. (Usually, when personally threatened with murder or rape, they change their tune!) Color-blind persons need help distinguishing red from green. Similarly, morally malfunctioning persons (those denying basic moral truths) don't need arguments; they need

* Originally published in the *CSB Apologetics Study Bible* under the same title.

psychological and spiritual help. Like logical laws, moral laws and instincts are basic to well-functioning humans.

As part of God's general self-revelation, all people—unless they ignore or suppress their conscience—can and should have basic moral insight, knowing truths generally available to any morally sensitive person (Rm 2:14–15). We instinctively recognize the wrongness of torturing or murdering the innocent or committing rape. We just know the rightness of virtues (kindness, trustworthiness, unselfishness). A person's failure to recognize these insights reveals something defective; he hasn't looked deeply enough into the grounds of his moral beliefs.

Philosophers and theologians past and present have noted the connection between God's existence and objective moral values. A moral argument for God's existence goes like this: (a) If objective moral values exist, then God exists. (b) Objective moral values do exist. (c) Therefore, God exists. If objective moral values exist, where do they come from? The most plausible answer is God's nature or character. Even many atheists have admitted that objective moral values (which they deny) don't fit an atheistic world but would serve as evidence for God's existence.

We live in a time when many claim everything is relative, yet ironically they believe they have "rights." But if morality is just the product of evolution, culture, or personal choice, then rights—and moral responsibility—do not truly exist. But if they *do,* this assumes humans have value in and of themselves as persons, no matter what their culture or science textbooks say. But what, then, is the basis for this value? Could this intrinsic value just emerge from impersonal, mindless, valueless processes over time (naturalism)?

An Eastern philosophical approach to ethics is monism (sometimes called "pantheism"): because everything is one, no ultimate distinction between good and evil exists. This serves to support relativism. A more natural context for ethics is the theistic one, in which we've been made by a good God to resemble him in certain important (though limited) ways. The Declaration of Independence correctly notes that we've been endowed by our Creator with "certain inalienable rights." Human dignity isn't just "there." Dignity and rights come from a good God (despite human sinfulness).

Can't atheists be moral? Yes! Like believers, they've been made in the image of God and thus have the ability to recognize right and wrong.

Doesn't God himself conform to certain moral standards outside himself? No, God's good character is the very standard; God simply acts and naturally does what is good. Universal moral standards have no basis if God doesn't exist.

CAN SOMETHING BE TRUE FOR YOU AND NOT FOR ME?*

Paul Copan

"It's all relative." "That's true for you but not for me." "That's just your reality." "Who are you to impose your values on others?" The relativist believes truth functions more like opinion or perspective and that truth depends upon your culture, context, or even personal choices. Thus evil actions by Nazis or terrorists are explained away ("We don't like it, but they have their reasons"). Relativism, however, is seriously flawed.

* Originally published in the *CSB Apologetics Study Bible* under the same title.

Relativism cannot escape proclaiming a truth that corresponds to reality. "The moon is made of cheese" is false because it does not match up with the way things are, with what is the case. As Christians, we claim the biblical story is true because it conforms to the actualities of God's existence and his dealings with human beings. Truth is a relationship—a match-up with what is real or actual. An idea is false when it does not. But what of those making such claims as "Reality is like a wet lump of clay—we can shape it any way we want" (a relativistic idea known as *antirealism*)? We can rightly call such statements into question. After all, these persons believe that their view corresponds to the way things are. If you disagree with them, they believe you are wrong. Notice, too, that they believe there is at least one thing that is not subject to human manipulation—namely, the unshakable reality that reality is like a wet lump of clay that we can shape any way we want to! So we can ask: "Is that lump-of-clay idea something you made up?" If it applies to everyone, then the statement is incoherent. If it doesn't, then it's nothing more than one's perspective. Why take it seriously? And if there's no objective truth or reality, how do we know that our beliefs are not delusional?

Relativism is self-contradictory. If someone claims to be a relativist, don't believe it. A relativist will say that your belief is true for you but his is true for him; there is no objective truth that applies to all people. The only problem is that this statement itself is an objective truth that applies to all people! (Even when he says, "That's true for you but not for me," he believes his view applies to more than just one person!) To show the self-contradictory nature of relativism, we can simply preface relativistic assertions this way: "It's objectively true that 'That's true for you but not for me'" or "It's true that 'There is no truth.'" The bold contradiction becomes apparent. Or what of the line that sincere belief makes something (Buddhism, Marxism, Christianity) true? We must ask, is this principle universal and absolute? Is it true even if I don't sincerely believe it? That is, what if I sincerely believe that sincere belief does not make something real? Both views obviously cannot be true.

The basis and conclusion of relativism are objectively true. Ask the relativist why she takes this view. She'll probably say, "So many people believe so many different things." The problem here is that she believes this to be universally true and beyond dispute. Furthermore, she believes that the logical conclusion to draw from the vast array of beliefs is that relativism must be the case. The relativist doesn't believe that all these different beliefs are a matter of personal preference. The basis for relativism (the variety of beliefs), and the conclusion that relativism obviously follows from it, turn out to be logical and objectively true for all people, not just the relativist!

Relativism will always be selective. People usually aren't relativists about the law of gravity, drug prescription labels, or the stock index. They're usually relativists when it comes to God's existence, sexual morality, or cheating on exams. But try cutting in line in front of a relativist, helping yourself to his property, or taking a sledgehammer to his car, and you will find out that he believes his rights have been violated! Rights and relativism don't mix. But if "it's all relative," why get mad at anyone?

Relativism is usually motivated by a personal agenda—the drive for self-control. Atheist philosopher

John Searle uncovers what's behind relativism: "It satisfies a basic urge to power. It just seems too disgusting, somehow, that we should have to be at the mercy of the 'real world.'" We want to be in charge. Now, pointing out one's motivation is not an argument against relativism; still, it's a noteworthy consideration. Truth often takes a backseat to freedom. But clearly, when a person shrugs off arguments for the inescapability of objective truth with "Whatever," he has another agenda in mind. Relativism makes no personal demands upon us—to love God, to be people of integrity, to help improve society. Even if relativism is false, it is convenient.

IF GOD MADE THE UNIVERSE, WHO MADE GOD?*

Paul Copan

Atheist philosopher Bertrand Russell mused, "If everything must have a cause, then God must have a cause." But the question of what or who caused God is misguided.

First, science supports the notion that the universe had a beginning and that something independent of the universe brought it into being. The well-accepted scientific belief in the universe's origination and expansion and the second law of thermodynamics

* Originally published in the *CSB Apologetics Study Bible* under the same title.

(energy tends to spread out) support the universe's absolute beginning from nothing. This sounds remarkably like Genesis 1:1! The chances of a thing's popping into being from literally nothing are exactly zero. Being cannot come from nonbeing; there's no potential for this. Even skeptic David Hume called this "absurd"—a scientific (real) impossibility.

Second, believers reject the claim "Everything that exists has a cause" and affirm "Whatever begins to exist has a cause." To say "Everything needs a cause" would necessarily exclude an uncaused God. This is "question begging" (assuming what needs to be proved). It's like presuming that since all reality is physical (which can't be demonstrated), a nonphysical God cannot exist.

Third, why think everything needs a cause, since an uncaused entity is logical and intelligible? Through the centuries, many believed that the universe didn't need a cause; it was self-existent. They thought a beginningless/uncaused universe wasn't illogical or impossible.

But now that contemporary cosmology points to the universe's beginning and an external cause, skeptics insist everything needs a cause after all!

Fourth, a good number of uncaused things exist. Logical laws are real; we can't think coherently without using them (e.g., the law of identity, X = X, tells you: "This book is this book"). Moral laws or virtues (love, justice) are real. But none of these began to exist. They are eternal and uncaused (being in God's mind).

Fifth, the question "Who made God?" commits the category fallacy. To say that all things, even God, must be caused is incoherent—like the question "How does the color green taste?" Why fault God for being uncaused? When we rephrase the question to say, "What caused the self-existent, uncaused Cause, who is by definition unmade, to exist?" the answer is obvious.

IS THE OLD TESTAMENT TRUSTWORTHY?*

Walter C. Kaiser Jr.

What is a modern reader of the Old Testament to do with a book that teaches animal sacrifice, male circumcision, strange dietary codes, and festivals based on an agricultural cycle? Its contents appear to be so ancient and so removed from our day that some dismiss it as "primitive religion."

Contrary to such a premature judgment, seven affirmations show that the Old Testament is at once relevant and altogether trustworthy.

* Originally published in the *CSB Apologetics Study Bible* under the same title.

1. ***In every part of the Old Testament the writers claim the divine origin of their writings.*** One such inspired utterance comes from the core of the Old Testament: the Ten Commandments. "Stone tablets inscribed by the finger of God" (Ex 31:18; cmp. Dt 5:22). More regularly, however, "the Spirit of the LORD spoke through [his prophets], his word was on [their] tongue[s]" (2Sm 23:2). Indeed, Nathan the prophet knew that he had spoken his own words, which were not the same as the words from divine revelation. When he spoke God's message, he prefaced it, as did the Old Testament prophets repeatedly, with "This is what the LORD says" (2Sm 7:5). Even in the wisdom books of the Old Testament, Agur introduced himself as deficient and ignorant. He complained, "I am more stupid than any other person, and I lack a human's ability to understand. I have not gained wisdom, and I have no knowledge of the Holy One" (Pr 30:2–3). How, then, would he know how or what to write about God? He asked the same questions in verse 4. But by verses 5–6 he had the answer: "Every word of God is pure . . . Don't add to his words, or he will rebuke you, and you will be proved a

liar." The first part of verse 5 is a quote from Psalm 18:30, while verse 6 is a quote from Deuteronomy 4:2.

2. ***The thirty nine books of the Old Testament were immediately received as authoritative and canonical (belonging to Scripture).*** One of the most popular misconceptions is that a group of scholars held a rabbinical council in Jamnia in AD 90 to decide which books they would regard as authoritative for composing the Old Testament. But this is incorrect: for (1) the council's decisions had no binding authority; (2) the discussions at that council were merely about the correct interpretations of the Ecclesiastes and Song of Songs; and (3) the list of books they regarded as canonical were already treated as the same thirty nine books in our current Old Testament. Instead, the books of the Old Testament were progressively recognized by those closest to the writers of the Old Testament as being indeed revelation from God. Daniel, writing about seventy-five years after the prophet Jeremiah, regarded his prophecy about the seventy-year captivity (Jr 25:11–12) as "the word of the Lord" (Dn 9:2). In fact, he placed the book

of Jeremiah among "the books," that is, in the group of books called the Scriptures.

3. ***The text of the Old Testament books was uniquely preserved when compared with other ancient writings.*** Prior to the discovery of the Dead Sea Scrolls in 1947, we were limited to the Greek text of the Septuagint, the Samaritan Pentateuch, and the Hebrew text of the Nash Papyrus dating from around AD 1000 for checking on the accuracy of the preservation of the Old Testament text. That has all changed. In the eight hundred exemplars of Old Testament biblical texts in the Dead Sea Scrolls, we now possess texts from 250 BC to AD 50. Moreover, the earliest example of an Old Testament text is Numbers 6:24–26 from the mid-seventh century BC in the Ketef Hinnom Plaques. So carefully preserved are these texts that when scholars studied the Dead Sea Scroll of Isaiah, only three minor spelling changes (comparable to the difference between spelling "Saviour" and "Savior") were found in a text that covers about one hundred pages in many English translations. That is an outstanding record of preserving the text of the Bible, which represents over a thousand years of copying the text.

4. ***The historical chronology found in the histories of the kings of Israel and Judah is completely verified and trustworthy.*** If chronology is the backbone of history, then it was necessary for someone to untangle the dates and systems of correlation between the kings of northern Israel and Judah if any confidence, much less sense, was to come out of these scores of numbers in the books of Kings and Chronicles. But that is what Edwin Thiele did as his doctoral dissertation for the University of Chicago. He first established as an absolute date (on our Julian calendar) June 15, 763 BC, from the astronomical citations on the Assyrian Eponym, or Man of the Year, lists. These annual lists also made allusions to several of the Hebrew kings, thereby providing excellent synchronisms. From there he was able to show how some five hundred numbers (all except one, which was later solved) were easily reconciled and totally trustworthy in every detail.

5. ***Archaeology has helped to show that the culture, persons, and events of the Old Testament are trustworthy.*** Archaeology has done much to further the cause of showing the reliability of the Old Testament.

Where there were alleged missing persons mentioned in the Old Testament, but not known from external sources, such as King Sargon in Isaiah 20:1, or Governor Sanballat of Samaria (Neh 2:10), or kings David, Ahab, Jehu, and Hezekiah, Menahem, and even a prophet, Balaam, in each case spectacular finds have vindicated the claims of the biblical text. In like manner, where the Old Testament claimed there were peoples such as the Hittites or the Horites, later finds vindicated the presence of these as well as other allegedly missing peoples. A similar list of allegedly missing places could be gathered, such as the land of Ophir or the sites along the Transjordanian route of the wilderness wanderings. But once again archaeology has given great help. This is not to say that all of those people and places alleged to have been created by the Old Testament have been fully identified. For example, we still cannot find external validation for Darius the Mede (Dn 5:31). But the success of archaeology in the twentieth century alone is startling in its extent and in the depth of its influence.

6. ***The present literary form of the books comes to us from ancient times and in the final shape in which we***

presently possess them. No section of the Old Testament has received more critical dissecting than the first five books of Moses, the Pentateuch. It was alleged that the books did not come by divine inspiration to Moses around 1400 BC but rather came from the hands of at least four main compilers (called J, E, D, and P) ranging from the eighth century BC, with the final hand and the final re-editing coming in 400 BC! At the heart of this theory was the book of Deuteronomy, which critical scholars claimed was first written in 621 BC, when King Josiah found the book of the law. But Deuteronomy exhibits the literary format that is unique to the middle of the second millennium BC Hittite suzerainty treaties (ca 1200–1400 BC), the same six sections of those treaties being found in the book of Deuteronomy. Had Deuteronomy been compiled in the first millennium (621 BC), as the critics claim, it would resemble instead the Assyrian treaties that had by that time deleted two of the six sections. Thus, according to the literary forms and criteria of the critics themselves, the key book in the disputed first five books must be placed in the days when Moses lived (i.e., around 1400 BC).

7. ***The writers of the Old Testament were aware that they were writing not only for their generation but also for those who would come later.*** The most convenient way to demonstrate this is to go to 1 Peter 1:12, where Peter stated, "It was revealed to [the prophets of the OT] that they were not serving themselves but you [people of Peter's generation and us]."

IS THE OLD TESTAMENT ETHICAL?*

Christopher Wright

The prevailing prejudice against Scripture is that the Old Testament portrays a violent God of a violent people and is filled with narratives recounting horrendous events with disreputable people playing major roles. Is the Old Testament ethical? Here are some reasons why it is.

It was ethical enough for Jesus. Jesus accepted the truth and ethical validity of the Old Testament ("the Scriptures") in his own life, mission, and teaching. His noted "you have heard that it was said . . . but I tell you"

* Originally published in the *CSB Apologetics Study Bible* under the same title.

(see Mt 5) sayings don't contradict or criticize the Old Testament but either deepen its demands or correct distorted popular inferences. "Love your neighbor" meant "Hate your enemy" to many in Jesus's day, even though the Old Testament never says any such thing. Jesus reminded his hearers that the same chapter (Lv 19) also says, "Love [the alien] as yourself," extending this to include "Love your enemy" (Mt 5:44). Jesus thus affirmed and strengthened the Old Testament ethic.

Narratives describe what happened, not what was necessarily approved. We assume wrongly that if a story is in Scripture it must be "what God wanted." But biblical narrators dealt with the real world and described it as it was, with all its corrupt and fallen ambiguity. We shouldn't mistake realism for ethical approval. Old Testament stories often challenge us to wonder at God's amazing grace and patience in continually working out his purpose through such morally compromised people and to be discerning in evaluating their conduct according to standards the Old Testament itself provides.

The conquest of Canaan must be understood for what it was. This event, rightly, is troubling to sensitive readers.

We can't ignore its horror, but some perspectives can help us evaluate it ethically.

- ***It was a limited event.*** The conquest narratives describe one particular period of Israel's long history. Many of the other wars that occur in the Old Testament narrative had no divine sanction, and some were clearly condemned as the actions of proud, greedy kings or military rivals.
- ***We must allow for the exaggerated language of warfare.*** Israel, like other ancient Near East nations whose documents we possess, had a rhetoric of war that often exceeded reality.
- ***It was an act of God's justice and punishment on a morally degraded society.*** The conquest shouldn't be portrayed as random genocide or ethnic cleansing. The wickedness of Canaanite society was anticipated (Gn 15:16) and described in moral and social terms (Lv 18:24; 20:23; Dt 9:5; 12:29–31). This interpretation is accepted in the New Testament (e.g., Heb 11:31 speaks of the Canaanites as "those who disobeyed," implying awareness of choosing to persist in sin—as the Bible affirms of all human

beings). There's a huge moral difference between violence that's arbitrary and violence inflicted within the moral framework of punishment (this is true in human society as much as in divine perspective). It doesn't make it "nice," but it changes the ethical evaluation significantly.

- ***God threatened to do the same to Israel—and he did.*** In the conquest God used Israel as the agent of punishment on the Canaanites. God warned Israel that if they behaved like the Canaanites, he would treat them as his enemy in the same way and inflict the same punishment on them using other nations (Lv 26:17; Dt 28:25–68). In the course of Israel's long history in Old Testament times, God repeatedly did so, demonstrating his moral consistency in international justice. It wasn't a matter of favoritism. If anything, Israel's status as God's chosen people, the Old Testament argues, exposed them more to God's judgment and historical punishment than the Canaanites who experienced the conquest. Those choosing to live as God's enemies eventually face God's judgment.

- ***The conquest anticipated the final judgment.*** Like the stories of Sodom and Gomorrah and the flood, the story of Canaan's conquest stands in Scripture as a prototypical narrative, or one that foreshadows what is to come. Scripture affirms that ultimately, in the final judgment, the wicked will face the awful reality of God's wrath through exclusion, punishment, and destruction. Then God's ethical justice will finally be vindicated. But at certain points in history, such as during the conquest period, God demonstrates the power of his judgment. Rahab's story, set in the midst of the conquest narrative, also demonstrates the power of repentance, faith, and God's willingness to spare his enemies when they choose to identify with God's people. Rahab thus enters the New Testament hall of fame—and faith (Heb 11:31; Jms 2:25).

An eye for an eye is remarkably humane. Unfortunately this phrase sums up for many what Old Testament law and ethics are all about. Even then they misunderstand that this expression—almost certainly metaphorical, not literal—wasn't a license for unlimited vengeance but precisely the opposite: it established the fundamental legal principle of proportionality; that is, punishment mustn't exceed the gravity of the offense. The rest of Old Testament law, when compared with law codes from contemporary ancient societies (e.g., Babylonian, Assyrian, Hittite), shows a remarkable humanitarian concern, especially for the socially weak, poor, and marginalized (the classic trio of "the widow, the orphan, and the alien"). Israel's laws operated with ethical priorities of human life above material property and of human needs over legal rights. Not surprisingly, then, Jesus (who clearly endorsed the same priorities) could affirm that he had no intention of abolishing the Law and the Prophets but rather of fulfilling them.

IS THE NEW TESTAMENT TRUSTWORTHY?*

Darrell L. Bock

Like any ancient book, the New Testament (NT) has a strange feel about it. It reports unusual events as well as strange customs. This naturally raises the question of whether we can trust what it tells us. These six statements of fact affirm that the NT can be trusted.

1. ***The books of the NT were recognized through a careful sifting process.*** The process stretched from the first to the fourth century. The catalysts for the formation of the NT were the use of Scripture in worship, the rise

* Originally published in the *CSB Apologetics Study Bible* under the same title.

of false teaching (which necessitated identifying the authentic works), and persecution (which called for the burning of holy books—so one needed to know which those were!). The books included in the NT were those regarded as giving evidence of divine authority. Was it associated with an apostle? Was it in line with other authentic biblical books? Was it widely used and received? These were the questions used to identify the trustworthy and authoritative books of the NT.

2. ***The NT is based on reliable sources carefully used and faithfully transmitted.*** The Bible is both like other books and unlike them. Luke explained that he used sources (Lk 1:1–4). Jesus taught that the Spirit would help these apostles recall what Jesus taught them (Jn 14:25–26). To argue that the Bible is inspired by God does not dismiss the human elements that make up the book. What are the sources, and how were they handled? The texts surrounding Jesus stress the role of eyewitnesses as the root of the tradition (see Lk 1:2). An apostolic association ensured the account's credibility.

The distance between event and recording is not great—less than a lifetime, a small distance of time by ancient standards. For example, the first-century Roman historians Livy and Dionysius of Halicarnassus were centuries removed from many of the events they chronicled. Judaism depended on the ability to pass things on with care from one generation to the next, recounting events with care. This does not exclude some variation, as is obvious by comparing the Gospel accounts or parallel accounts in 1 and 2 Samuel, 1 and 2 Kings, and 1 and 2 Chronicles. Judaism, and the Christianity that grew out of it, was a culture of memory. People memorized long liturgical prayers and more often than not worked from memory rather than from a written page. Anyone who has read a children's book again and again to his child knows that the mind is capable of absorbing vast amounts of wording and retaining it.

Finally the biblical text we have today basically reflects the text as it was originally produced. The NT has far better manuscript evidence than any other ancient document. Where most classical works, such as those of Plato, Herodotus, and Aristophanes, have from one to twenty manuscripts, the NT has about 5,400 Greek manuscripts that we can compare to determine the original wording, not to mention more than 8,000 ancient Latin manuscripts.

3. ***Assessing trustworthiness means understanding history's complexity.*** Differences in accounts do not necessarily equal contradiction, nor does subsequent reflection mean a denial of history. Events can be viewed from different angles or perspectives without forfeiting historicity. Thus the differences in the four Gospels enrich our appreciation of Jesus by giving us four perspectives on him—Jesus in four dimensions, so to speak. Neither is reflection a denial of history. Sometimes the significance of a historical event, such as a football play, becomes clear only when we see successive events. History involves both what happened and its results. Trustworthiness simply affirms that the assessed account is an accurate portrayal of what took place and a credible explanation of what emerged, not that it is the only way the events in question were seen.

4. ***Trustworthiness demands not exhaustive but adequate knowledge of the topic.*** Sources are selective even when they are accurate. The Bible makes this point in John 21:25: "And there are also many other things that

Jesus did, which, if every one of them were written down, I suppose not even the world itself could contain the books that would be written." When people call Scripture trustworthy, they are arguing that its testimony is not contrary to what happened and is sufficient to give us a meaningful understanding of God and his work for us (2Tm 3:16–17). Speaking *accurately* is not the same as speaking *exhaustively*.

5. ***Archaeology teaches us to respect the content of Scripture.*** Archaeology seldom can prove that events took place. What it can show is that the details of an account, some of them incidental, fit the time and culture of the text. Archaeology also shows that we should be cautious in pointing out errors in the Bible merely because only the Bible attests to something.

For example, there was once debate about the description in John 5:2 of a pool with five porticoes in Jerusalem, called Bethesda or Bethsaida. Many questioned its existence despite its wide attestation in ancient tradition. Different spellings of the locale in the NT manuscript tradition added to the tendency by many to reject the claim. In 1871 a French architect, C. Mauss, was restoring an old church and found a cistern thirty meters away. Later excavations in 1957–1962 clarified that it consisted of two pools large enough to hold a sizable amount of water and people. Today virtually no one doubts the existence of John's pool.

6. ***The Bible's claim for miracles are plausible when one considers the response to resurrection claims.*** The events of the Gospels were recorded within the lifetime of several of those who claimed to have observed them. Perhaps the greatest evidence for the resurrection is the change and reaction of those who testified to it. They disciples openly admitted that they had no formal training and for a long period were shockingly inept at responding to Jesus. Yet they became courageous leaders. The stood firm in the face of the threat of death and rejection by the Jewish leaders who resisted them. This did not involve one or two people but a whole host of leaders who left their mark on history, notably the former chief persecutor of the church, Paul. Both Peter and he, along with others such as the Lord's brother James, died for their belief in Jesus's resurrection.

HAS HISTORICAL CRITICISM PROVED THE BIBLE FALSE?*

Thomas R. Schreiner

Historical criticism of the Bible began in earnest in the eighteenth century, flowered in the nineteenth century, and became the dominant approach to the Scriptures in the twentieth century. Historical criticism has at times been rejected by conservatives because it has called into question the accuracy of the Bible. For example, in the nineteenth century, most scholars delving into the life of Jesus provided rationalistic, not supernatural, explanations of Jesus's miracles. New

* Originally published in the *CSB Apologetics Study Bible* under the same title.

Testament scholar F. C. Baur argued that the theologies of Peter and Paul contradict one another if one reads the New Testament (NT) historically. Old Testament (OT) scholars, such as Julius Wellhausen, maintained that the Pentateuch (first five books of the Bible) was not actually written by Moses. Careful literary and historical study, it was claimed, indicated that the Pentateuch had various sources that were written over a period of hundreds of years and that the final document was put together by an unknown editor.

Still, it is important to recognize that the rise of historical criticism has also benefited the church. The Christian faith is rooted in history. God has manifested himself supremely in the person of Jesus Christ. He lived and ministered in a particular time and place—in Palestine in the third decade of the first century. As Christians, then, we believe that our faith is historically rooted. Paul insisted that Christians were foolish to believe in the Christian faith if the resurrection of Jesus did not actually occur (1Co 15:12–19). Hence, we have no fear of historical study but welcome it, for we believe historical research can assist us in understanding the message of the Scriptures.

The benefits of historical study are numerous. It has cleared up the meaning of obscure terms. The discovery of the Dead Sea Scrolls has cast light on the environment within which the NT was birthed. Study of the ancient Near East and the Greco-Roman world has clarified the extent to which the Scriptures are similar to and dissimilar from documents that came out of surrounding cultures. Historical criticism has also demonstrated that some traditional views were not credible. It was once thought that the NT was written in a special "Holy Ghost" language, but study of sources from the era of the NT has demonstrated that the NT was written in the common Greek of the day. The King James Version of the Bible was an outstanding product of the scholarship in its day, but we now have many more manuscripts for both the NT and the OT, and hence our English Bibles are even closer to the original today because of recent manuscript discoveries and the careful work of scholars in text criticism.

While historical criticism has benefited the church, it also carries with it liabilities. Many scholars who practiced historical criticism imbibed the Enlightenment philosophy sweeping Europe in the eighteenth and nineteenth centuries. Their philosophical worldview masqueraded as historical criticism. As described above, they rejected the miracles of Jesus and provided rationalistic explanations. But scholars do not reject miracles on historical grounds. They have accepted a naturalistic philosophical standpoint that presupposed that miracles don't happen. On this view, even impressive evidence to the contrary is beside the point. Rudolf Bultmann is an example of this view. Bultmann defined historical work in such a way that the acceptance of any miracles was excluded. When we read the NT, we see that credible historical reasons exist to support the resurrection of Christ, but many scholars refuse even to consider the evidence, for they are convinced from the start that resurrections cannot happen. This fundamental bias (i.e., naturalistic philosophy) is all too often cloaked as "objective history."

Historical criticism hoped that it would succeed where orthodoxy failed. In the sixteenth and seventeenth centuries, orthodox Christians debated the interpretation of the Bible, leading to several different theological systems (Lutheranism, Calvinism, Arminianism). Historical critics believed that they were more objective and that by means of a "neutral" scientific approach they could discover what the Bible really taught. But with the arrival of postmodernism this view seems naive to almost all scholars today. And the record of historical criticism reveals that it did not succeed in agreeing upon "the assured results of scholarship." Indeed, a dizzying array of viewpoints and perspectives are present in historical criticism today, and many of them are mutually contradictory.

The work of F. C. Baur and Julius Wellhausen threatened the faith of evangelical believers in the nineteenth century. Yet few scholars today embrace the conclusions of F. C. Baur, and the documentary hypothesis of Wellhausen is severely questioned. The "assured results" of scholarship in one generation are often vigorously challenged by the next. Evangelicals, of course, should be open to correction. Perhaps we have misread some parts of the Bible because of our tradition. On the other hand, we need to be critical and savvy and to reject the temptation of embracing the latest fad in scholarship just because it is current.

Though evangelical scholars have often solved problems raised by historical critics, conservatives have not solved them all. This does not mean that the Scriptures are inaccurate in such instances but instead that we could resolve such problems if we had enough information. To make such a claim is not a sacrifice of one's intellect. Comprehensive answers are lacking in every historical discipline since the evidence is fragmentary. We can be grateful to historical criticism since it has helped us understand the Scriptures better. But we must also be on our guard. Often historical criticism has veered off into unsubstantiated allegations about the accuracy of the Scriptures, and it has routinely approached the Scriptures with an anti-supernatural worldview. Historical criticism has not demonstrated the Bible to be false. The Bible, rightly interpreted, has stood the test of time.

ARE MIRACLES BELIEVABLE?*

Ronald H. Nash

Miracles are essential to the historic Christian faith. If Jesus Christ was not God incarnate, and if Jesus did not rise bodily from the grave, then the Christian faith as we know it from history and the Scriptures would not—could not—be true (see Rm 10:9–10). It is then, easy to see why enemies of the Christian faith direct many of their attacks against these two miracles of Christ's incarnation and resurrection in particular and against the possibility of miracles in general.

What one believes about the possibility of miracles

* Originally published in the *CSB Apologetics Study Bible* under the same title.

comes from that person's worldview. On the question of miracles, the critical worldview distinction is between naturalism and supernaturalism. For a naturalist, the universe is analogous to a closed box. Everything that happens inside the box is caused by, or is explicable in terms of, other things that exist within the box. *Nothing* (including God) exists outside the box; therefore, nothing outside the box we call the universe or nature can have any causal effect within the box. To quote the famous naturalist Carl Sagan, the cosmos is all that is or ever has been or ever will be. The major reason, then, why naturalists do not believe in miracles is because their worldview prevents them from believing.

If a naturalist suddenly begins to consider the possibility that miracles are really possible, he has begun to move away from naturalism and toward a different worldview. Any person with a naturalistic worldview could not consistently believe in miracles. No arguments on behalf of the miraculous can possibly succeed with such a person. The proper way to address the unbelief of such a person is to begin by challenging his naturalism.

The worldview of Christian theism affirms the existence

of a personal God who transcends nature, who exists "outside the box." Christian supernaturalism denies the eternity of nature. God created the world freely and *ex nihilo* (out of nothing). The universe is contingent in the sense that it would not have begun to exist without God's creative act and it could not continue to exist without God's sustaining activity. The very laws of the cosmos that naturalists believe make miracles impossible were created by this God. Indeed one of naturalism's major problems is explaining how mindless forces could give rise to minds, knowledge, and sound reasoning.

DID JESUS REALLY RISE FROM THE DEAD?*

William Lane Craig

To answer our question from a historical standpoint, we must first determine what facts concerning the fate of Jesus of Nazareth can be credibly established on the basis of the evidence and second consider what the best explanation of those facts is. At least four facts about the fate of the historical Jesus are widely accepted by New Testament historians today.

Fact 1: After his crucifixion, Jesus was buried by Joseph of Arimathea in a tomb. This fact is highly

* Originally published in the *CSB Apologetics Study Bible* under the same title.

significant because it means that the location of Jesus's tomb was known in Jerusalem to Jews and Christians alike. New Testament scholars have established the fact of Jesus's entombment on the basis of evidence such as the following:

1. Jesus's burial is attested in the information (from before AD 36) that was handed on by Paul in 1 Corinthians 15:3–5.
2. The burial story is independently attested in the source material that was used by Mark in writing his Gospel.
3. Given the understandable hostility in the early Christian movement toward the Jewish national leaders, Joseph of Arimathea, as a member of the Jewish high court that condemned Jesus, is unlikely to have been a Christian invention.
4. The burial story is simple and lacks any signs of being developed into a legend.
5. No other competing burial story exists.

For these and other reasons, the majority of New Testament critics concur that Jesus was in fact buried by Joseph of Arimathea in a tomb.

Fact 2: On the Sunday after the crucifixion, Jesus's tomb was found empty by a group of his women followers. Among the reasons that have led most scholars to this conclusion are the following:

1. In stating that Jesus "was buried, that he was raised on the third day," the old information transmitted by Paul in 1 Corinthians 15:3–5 implies the empty tomb.
2. The empty tomb story also has multiple and independent attestation in Mark, Matthew, and John's source material, some of which is very early.
3. The empty tomb story as related in Mark, our earliest account, is simple and lacks signs of having been embellished as a legend.
4. Given that in Jewish patriarchal culture the testimony of women was regarded as unreliable, the fact that women, rather than men, were the chief witnesses to the empty tomb is best explained by the narrative's being true.
5. The earliest known Jewish response to the proclamation of Jesus's resurrection, namely, the "disciples came during the night and stole him

while we were sleeping" (Mt 28:12–15), was itself an attempt to explain why the body was missing and thus presupposes the empty tomb.

For these and other reasons, a majority of scholars hold firmly to the reliability of the biblical testimony to Jesus's empty tomb.

Fact 3: On multiple occasions, and under various circumstances, different individuals and groups saw Jesus alive after his death. This fact is almost universally acknowledged among New Testament scholars for the following reasons:

1. Given its early date as well as Paul's personal acquaintance with the people involved, the list of eyewitnesses to Jesus's resurrection appearances that is quoted by Paul in 1 Corinthians 15:5–8 guarantees that such appearances occurred.
2. The appearance narratives in the Gospels provide multiple, independent attestations of the appearances.

Even the most skeptical critics acknowledge that the disciples had seen Jesus alive after his death.

Finally, fact 4: The original disciples suddenly and sincerely came to believe Jesus was risen from the dead, despite having every predisposition to the contrary. Consider the situation the disciples faced following Jesus's crucifixion:

1. Their leader was dead and Jewish messianic expectations did not expect a Messiah who, instead of triumphing over Israel's enemies, would be shamefully executed by them as a criminal.
2. According to Old Testament law, Jesus's execution exposed him as a heretic, a man accursed by God.
3. Jewish beliefs about the afterlife precluded anyone's rising from the dead to glory and immortality before the general resurrection of the dead at the end of the world.

Nevertheless, the original disciples suddenly came to believe so strongly that God had raised Jesus from the dead that they were willing to die for that belief.

We come now to our second concern: What is the best explanation of these four facts? In his book *Justifying Historical Descriptions,* historian C. B. McCullagh lists six tests historians use to determine the best explanation for a given body of historical facts. The hypothesis given by the eyewitnesses—"God raised Jesus from the dead"—passes all these tests:

1. ***It has great explanatory scope.*** It explains why the tomb was found empty, why the disciples saw postmortem appearances of Jesus, and why the Christian faith came into being.
2. ***It has great explanatory power.*** It explains why the body of Jesus was gone, why people repeatedly saw Jesus alive despite his earlier public execution, and so forth.
3. ***It is plausible.*** Given the historical context of Jesus's unparalleled life and claims, the resurrection makes sense as the divine confirmation of those radical claims.
4. ***It is not ad hoc or contrived.*** It requires only one additional hypothesis: that God exists.
5. ***It is in accord with accepted beliefs.*** The hypothesis "God raised Jesus from the dead" does not in any way conflict with the accepted belief that people do not rise naturally from the dead. The Christian

accepts that belief as wholeheartedly as he accepts the hypothesis that God raised Jesus from the dead.

6. ***It far outstrips any of its rival theories in meeting conditions 1 through 5.*** Down through history, various alternative explanations of the facts have been offered—the conspiracy theory, the apparent death theory, the hallucination theory, and so forth. Such hypotheses have been almost universally rejected by contemporary scholarship. No naturalistic hypothesis has, in fact, attracted a great number of scholars.

Therefore, the best explanation of the established facts seems to be that God raised Jesus from the dead.

We have firm historical grounds for answering our question in the affirmative. The historical route is not, however, the only avenue to a knowledge of Jesus's resurrection. The majority of Christians, who have had neither the resources, training, nor leisure to conduct a historical inquiry into this event, have come to a knowledge of Jesus's resurrection through a personal encounter with the living Lord (Rm 8:9–17).

CAN NATURALISTIC THEORIES ACCOUNT FOR THE RESURRECTION?*

Gary R. Habermas

One of our first thoughts when we hear someone claim to have witnessed a miracle is that there must be some sort of natural explanation. After all, even if they do occur, miracles are not the norm in nature.

In the Gospels we are told there was a similar response relating to Christ's resurrection. When the Jewish priests were told the report of the empty tomb, they spread the tale that Jesus's disciples had stolen his body (Mt 28:12–15).

* Originally published in the *CSB Apologetics Study Bible* under the same title.

Even believers reacted this way. When Mary Magdalene initially saw Jesus, she made a natural assumption, supposing he was the gardener (Jn 20:10–15). When the disciples heard the report of the women who had gone to Jesus's tomb, they thought the women were spreading rumors or false tales (Lk 24:11). Later, when they saw the risen Jesus, these same followers thought they were seeing a ghost or hallucination (Lk 24:36–43).

Throughout history many have had similar responses regarding Jesus's resurrection, attempting to come up with naturalistic theories to explain away the resurrection. These attempts were far more common in the nineteenth century than they are today. Even if we were to ignore the majority of the information in the Gospels, appealing only to those historical facts that are acknowledged by virtually every scholar who studies this subject, both conservative and liberal, we still have many major responses to each of the naturalistic theories. Not surprisingly, comparatively few scholars today think any of these alternative hypotheses really works.

For example, few critics have proposed that Jesus never died on the cross but instead "swooned"—fainted and only appeared dead. Dozens of medical studies have shown how death by crucifixion really kills and how this would be recognized by those present. Most of these reports argue that the chief cause of death in crucifixion was asphyxiation (death from being unable to breathe). It is even easy to ascertain when the victim was dead—he remained hanging in the down position without pushing up to breathe. Additionally, a death blow frequently ensured the victim's demise. The prevailing medical explanation of Jesus's chest wound is that the presence of blood and water indicated he was stabbed through the heart, thereby ensuring his death.

But many scholars think another serious problem dooms the swoon theory. If Jesus had not died on the cross, he would have been in exceptionally bad shape when his followers saw him. Limping profusely, bleeding from his many wounds and probably even leaving a bloody trail, stoop-shouldered and pale, he hardly would have been able to convince his disciples that he was their risen Lord—and in a transformed body at that! Many historical reasons and the near unanimity of scholarly opinion indicate that Jesus's disciples at least truly believed they had seen him resurrected. On such grounds the swoon thesis is actually self-refuting. It presents a Jesus who would have contradicted the disciples' belief in his resurrection simply by appearing in the horrible physical shape that is demanded by this view!

But could the disciples have stolen his dead body? This approach has been almost ignored for more than two hundred years because it would not explain the disciples' sincere belief that they had seen the risen Jesus—a belief for which they were clearly willing to die. Their transformations need an adequate explanation. Neither would the theft hypothesis explain the conversions from skepticism by James, the brother of Jesus, or Paul, occasioned by their own beliefs that they had also seen the risen Jesus. These facts are noted even by critical scholars.

Might someone else have stolen Jesus's body? This approach addresses nothing but the empty tomb. It provides no explanation for Jesus's appearances, which are the best evidence for the resurrection. Further, it fails to account for the conversions of James and Paul. Besides, many candidates for the body stealers would have had no motivation for taking the body. This alternative accounts for far too little of the known data. It is no wonder that critics virtually never opt for it.

There are myriads of problems with hallucination theories, too. We will mention just a few. Hallucinations are private experiences, whereas our earliest accounts report that Jesus appeared to groups as well as to individuals. Further, the dissimilar personalities witnessing the appearances clearly militate against everyone's inventing a mental image, often at the same time. So do the reactions of those disciples who responded to reports of the resurrection by doubting. The conversions of James and Paul are extremely problematic for this view, since unbelieving skeptics would hardly desire to hallucinate about the risen Jesus. And if hallucinations are the best explanation, then the tomb should not have been empty!

Could the resurrection accounts have developed later as mere stories that grew over time? A few of the potential responses should be adequate. Here again, the fact that the disciples truly believed they had seen the risen Jesus is highly problematic for this view, since it indicates the original accounts were derived from the eyewitnesses themselves, not from some later stories. Further, the fact that these appearances were reported extremely early, within just a few years of the crucifixion, attests that at least the core message was intact from the outset. Moreover, the empty tomb would be a constant physical reminder that this was not just some ungrounded tale. Both James and Paul again provide even more insurmountable problems for this view, for these skeptics were convinced that they had also seen the risen Jesus; tales developing years later fail to account for their conversions.

For reasons such as these, most critical scholars today reject the naturalistic theories as adequate accounts of Jesus's resurrection. They simply do not explain the known historical data. In fact, many liberal scholars even critique the alternatives that are periodically suggested!

Here we have a strong witness to the historical nature of Jesus's resurrection. Naturalistic theories have failed. Further, many historical evidences favor the resurrection. Taking all this together, we have strong reasons to believe that this event actually occurred in history. After all, the more thoroughly the alternative theories fail, the more we are left with the evidences themselves, and they are powerful indicators that Jesus rose from the dead.

THE APOLOGETICS STUDY BIBLE

REAL QUESTIONS.STRAIGHT ANSWERS. STRONGER FAITH.

APOLOGETICS STUDY BIBLE FOR STUDENTS

Edited by Dr. Sean McDowell

ApologeticsBible.com